Old LASSWADE & BONN

by

Oliver Van Helden

Elm Row, Lasswade.

When there was nae Brig, to cross the Esk River.
On Jeney's braid back they a'gaed the gither,
For Jeney was honest, stout, sober & steady,
She carried the Laird, she carried his Leddy,
When he was richt seated the doggie first gaed,
Then waving his stick he cried "Jenny Lass, Wade"

(Origin of the name of the Village of Lasswade.)

"Jenny Lass Wade"

Although the practice of women, and occasionally men, carrying wayfarers across river fords in the Middle Ages was apparently once common and regarded as an act of piety, the story about Jenny bearing the laird across the North Esk is spurious. Instead, Lasswade is thought to derive either from the Anglo-Saxon laes (a common) and weyde (a meadow), giving 'a common meadow'; or from the Gaelic leas (a fold) and bhead (a wood), giving . . . a fold at a wood!

Introduction

Originally separate settlements, Lasswade and Bonnyrigg expanded dramatically during the nineteenth century as their burgeoning industries created employment for an ever-increasing workforce. In 1929 they were amalgamated into a joint burgh and are now physically joined together.

Lasswade was initially the larger and more prosperous settlement. Bonnyrigg, in the neighbouring parish of Cockpen, remained a small collier village until well into the nineteenth century, and even by the 1860s was centred around only four streets, 'not closely built nor thickly populated'. By contrast, as early as 1697 Lasswade's inhabitants were boasting that they lived in 'no obscure parish'. With the main road southwards to Berwick upon Tweed and Newcastle passing through the village, Lasswade was both accessible to the capital, while at the same time very much in the country.

Natural resources within the parish bounds include coal deposits, fertile agricultural land and the River North Esk. This variety of resources allowed Lasswade to develop a diverse economic base, and prompted one historian to describe it as 'an economically and socially precocious parish . . . not typical perhaps of the largely agricultural, subsistence communities said to characterise pre-industrial Scotland'. At the end of the 1690s it was home to 90 tradesmen including mealmakers, millers, weavers, tailors, wrights, smiths, brewers and merchants.

Proximity to Edinburgh had a number of benefits. For one, it gave access to a giant market place where goods fetched city prices. The Rev. John Paton, author of the First Statistical Account, observed that the parish's average annual coal production of 30,000 tons was valued at £6,000 to £7,000 at the pit head but worth £12,000 to £14,000 when delivered to Edinburgh.

During the eighteenth century, Lasswade developed a thriving manufacturing base which encouraged a significant influx of workers. The local economy diversified into new industries and this was largely catalysed by events that were taking place in Edinburgh. By the middle of the eighteenth century, the capital had established itself as a major centre for printing and publishing and with a corresponding growth in dependent trades paper-making became an important industry in the Leith and Esk valleys. Edinburgh was also a source of entrepreneurial cash for the establishment of the new industries.

Between 1755 and 1791 the parish's population increased from 2,190 to over 3,000. Commenting on this Rev. Paton observed that 'improvements of every kind have been carried on to a great extent, which has occasioned a gread demand for labourers.' Alexander Campbell, writing in his Journey From Edinburgh through Parts of North Britain in 1802, noted that 'There are barley and meal mills, five paper mills, and two bleach fields in or near the populous village.'

Whilst the banks of the North Esk were being turned into a giant industrial estate, Bonnyrigg remained a small village consisting of a few isolated groups of cottages. Mining in the area became increasingly important and well organised as the nineteenth century progressed, encouraging a greater degree of settlement above Lasswade, but another major factor in Bonnyrigg's development was the relocation there of Lasswade's carpet factory.

Having moved from Edinburgh to Lasswade in 1834, Richard Whytock's carpet manufacturing business was forced to find new premises when Lord Melville, owner of the land on which the factory stood, refused to renew its lease. This decision was made to honour a promise made by Melville to the Duke of Buccleugh, who had complained about waste from the factory polluting the Esk, which flowed through the grounds of his residence, Dakeith House. Trading as Henry Widnell and Sons (Richard Whytock had retired some years previously), the jilted company immediately established two new factories elsewhere south of Dalkeith, but as the Esk flows northwards the pollution continued.

This was a significant stroke of luck for Bonnyrigg. Recalling life in the burgh during the 1860s, ex-provost George Brown commented in 1925 that 'the carpet factory then as now was a great asset to the town and district providing as it has always done good steady employment to so large a section of the community. It has been a great factor in the prosperity of the burgh.'

Meanwhile, Lasswade's fortunes were in decline. The village's situation on the North Esk, along which the early grain and paper mills had been established, was no longer an asset. Instead, as the traditional industries became mechanised and the need for water power declined, the location in a narrow valley accessible only by steep winding roads became a restriction. Lasswade had no space to expand. Bonnyrigg, positioned on higher open ground, grew as a result. Writing in the Third Statistical Account of 1955, J. Napier Hutchison observed that 'since the First World War, and particularly since the Second War, hundreds of houses have been erected in the parish, many in Bonnyrigg itself, but only five . . . in Lasswade village, which more and more presents a spectacle of desolation.' Heavy traffic on its twisting roads has made present day Lasswade High Street and Bridgend no-go areas for pedestrians -the 'quaintly irregular village' has now lost much of its rural charm. Only amongst the Victorian villas of Broomieknowe and Hillhead, away from the hazards of the A768, can the village's original attractions be appreciated. Bonnyrigg, the busier end of the burgh, has a healthy commercial centre and a fairly prosperous community, many of whom work in Edinburgh. Lasswade has never fully recovered from the demise of the paper mills and itsother industries, but also benefits today from a rural setting within easy reach of the city.

Main Street, Lasswade.

Lasswade from the Edinburgh road. The building with the pointed facade is the only one left standing and houses the laundrette. Behind the buildings on the left Richard Whytock of Edinburgh established his St Anne's carpet factory on the banks of the North Esk in 1834 in a former brewery. The factory produced bespoke carpets of different shapes and sizes without seams, as well as a new line called tapestry carpet which Whytock had patented in 1832. St Anne's employed over 100 people and in 1848 had 50 looms.

High Street. Lasswade.

M. 281

Looking away from the centre of Lasswade to the Edinburgh road during the depressed 1930s.

LASSWADE FROM ESKSIDE

In the early seventeeth century the inhabitants of Lasswade organised a petition to allow them to charge a toll at the bridge. There were complaints that 'the bridge of Lesswaid is become so ruynous that, yf some speedy remeid be not provydit for repairing thairof, it will not faill altogidder to perrishe and decay'. Despite this the same grumbles were being expressed almost twenty years later.

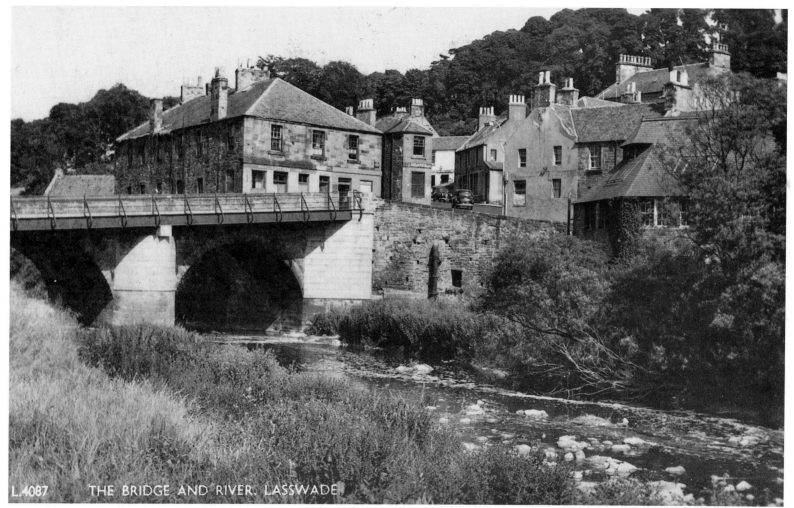

L.4087   THE BRIDGE AND RIVER. LASSWADE

With the advent of motor transport, Lasswade's narrow, elderly bridge became a dangerous bottleneck in the village and although the Third Statistical Account of 1955 mentions plans for a bypass to be built over the Middle Mills Valley 'within twenty years', these never transpired.

Middle Mills lies just to the north of Lasswade, beyond the park, and was a meal mill which once supplied the royal family in London. A map of 1866 shows a lade leading from Bridgend and through Lasswade Park to Middle Mill now the site of the road through the park.

31/10/02

I send you a view of your old quarters, & hope you are not wishing you were back again. Are you keeping in mind that I am open to accept a good job out beside you, anything from a baker to a minister or a missionary. would suit me, perhaps the latter would be best. Let me know when you are getting married, & if you want one from this district I will be most happy to bring her out to you.

There is nothing stirring going on here just now except the church dispute. If you should meet any heiresses out there, you might put in a word for me. Lily says she would like a husband too.

R.B.

This chemist's shop, which stood by the bridge, was reputedly the second oldest in Scotland. Its prescription book included entries referring to medicines collected by the writer Thomas De Quincey, although whether these were for the opium he was addicted to is not clear. This postcard was sent to a gentleman in Cathcart, Cape Colony, and appears to be from a lady seeking a husband and a job out there read: 'If you should meet any business out there, you might put in a word for me. Lily says she would like a husband too. R.B.'

THE BRIDGE. LASSWADE

From the eighteenth century onwards, Lasswade and its environs were renowned for their beauty. In 1791 John Paton described the North Esk as having 'a most beautiful run for several miles within this parish', circumstances that had attracted alongside it 'a constant succession of gentleman's seats, many of them large and excellent houses'. But by the 1950s both Lasswade and the river that made it prosperous had seen better days. In 1955 the village was described as being in 'a state of utter dereliction', and the North Esk 'much polluted by discharge from paper mills and pits along almost the whole of its length'.

The North Esk from Lasswade Bridge. School Green (on the right) was traditionally a gathering place and playground for village children, and long-forgotten games such as giddy-goat, cat-and-bat and cockertie-hooie were once played there. In 1953 local bookseller J.B. Cairns wrote that 'the schoolgreen and the banks and bed of the River Esk are now in a shocking state of neglect'. Previously, he remembered the green as the venue for travelling shows, including one boasting 'The Greatest Travelling Collection of Waxworks ever seen in this Country'. The outhouses on the river bank - believed to be farm buildings - no longer exist, although the cottages behind them are still standing.

LASSWADE AND CHURCH

The view across the North Esk to Lasswade Parish Church, with the bollards of the School Green in the foreground. In 1802 Alexander Campbell wrote 'the banks of the Esk about this village are well adapted to the cultivation of strawberries: a Scottish acre is often known to yield, in remarkable good seasons, from 36 to 40 pound sterling in value.' John Paton also mentions strawberry growing in the 1790s First Statistical Account, commenting not only on the high value of the crop but also on its dependability, adding that 'it was in this parish that strawberries were first raised in any quantities for the public market.'

Elm Row Lasswade.

M. 281

Most of the buildings on Elm Row, which leads away from Lasswade bridge and towards Dalkeith, have been demolished. The two-storey building on the corner of the junction with Polton Road (the ground floor is painted white) still stands and is occupied by Howden and Welton Motor Engineers.

Elm Road, Lasswade.

The devastation continues further up the street. The substantial building in the foreground has survived but with bricked-up doors and windows sits forlornly and alone, surrounded by the car park and scrap yard that now occupy the site of its neighbours. The building is unlikely to survive.

THE BRIDGE, LASSWADE.

During heavy rains in September 1891, the tall turreted Old Bank Buildings on the left of this picture were flooded. The Dalkeith Advertiser reported that the buildings were 'inundated to a depth of nearly three feet, and it became a matter of great difficulty to pump the water away. In fact the water flowed in faster than it was got rid of, until Mr Tod of St Leonard's Mill sent assistance to the inmates of the house.' The mill across the river was also put in danger: 'Large masses of the embankment were swept away by the force of the water, and the St Leonard's Paper Mill was flooded and work suspended at an early hour in the day.'

POLTON ROAD, LASSWADE.

Lasswade Parish Church (until recently Strathesk Church) was built in 1830 as the United Presbyterian Church but eventually became part of the Church of Scotland. Shortly after renovations to the building in 1894, the congregation held a fund-raising bazaar for which 'a very liberal supply of valuable goods of all kinds was furnished.' Attractions at the bazaar, held in Bonnyrigg Public Hall, included a shooting gallery, fish pond, tableaux vivants, and an orchestra. £337 was raised, a useful contribution towards the cost of improvements which included the addition of a porch and bell, and hearing tubes for the deaf. Incidentally, John Tod, Lasswade paper merchant, once likened the shape of the U.P. church to 'a weel clappit cairt o' dung'!

In 1793 a new parish church was built to replace its dilapidated medieval predecessor, but by the 1950s was described as having 'fallen upon evil days'. Extensive dry rot and woodworm made its 1956 demolition inescapable. The displaced congregation joined Strathesk Church on Polton Road. Ironically, a substantial portion of the medieval church still stands.

The runic cross was erected to Dr Richard Smith of Lasswade and his son. Dr Smith practised locally for over 45 years, riding a shaggy brown pony called Paddy on visits to patients. His son, also called Richard, was a hero of the Indian Mutiny.

L.4083 LASSWADE

In recent years small private housing developments have filled many corners of Lasswade, and the grassy area in the foreground is now the site of Cuguen Place, named after the mayor of Saint-Cyr, the burgh's French twin town. Shortly after they were built, some of the properties couldn't resist the pull of gravity and began slipping down the steep hillside that they were built on. Affected residents were offered alternative accomodation while their houses were shored up and the remedial work carried out. The two storey wooden building on the left of the picture is one of only ten houses that were built in Lasswade between the thirties and fifties - hundreds were built in Bonnyrigg during the same period.

Lasswade From The Viaduct.

M. 281.

From the middle of the eighteenth century, Lasswade's growth and development was intimately associated with paper making. In 1791 John Paton noted that the number of people employed in the industry had increased from 30 or 40 to about 260 over the previous 30 years. By 1845, the number of mills had dropped to three, but 'in all of these, machines are at work day and night, and the quantity of paper made is immense.' The giant chimney belonged to St Leonard's Mill, which was established on the North Esk in 1843. At 272 feet was the tallest structure for miles around and a prominent landmark.

Lasswade looking eastwards across the North Esk (the river is hidden in the dip of the valley). As the picture opposite shows, water from the river was once diverted at this point to form a reservoir called St Leonard's Pond, with a narrow channel of water next to it forming the Mill Lead (Lade). The reservoir has since been drained and, along with the grassy area in this picture, is now the site of Kevock Vale Park Home Estate, a substantial collection of prefab houses and fixed caravans.

The Viaduct. Lasswade.

M. 281

In 1861 the Esk Valley Railway established a branch line from the Edinburgh to Peebles line to Polton, with intermediate stops at Broomieknowe and Lasswade. The line entered a 471 yard tunnel between Broomieknowe and Lasswade stations, and then continued over the viaduct. Lasswade Station stood at the eastern end of the viaduct to the left of this picture, between Westmill Road and Polton Road. A gas works, probably the Lasswade and Bonnyrigg Gas-Light Co. Ltd, is visible just to the left of the station. The gas holder on the other side of the viaduct was a balancing tank for the national gas grid.

Lasswade From The Station.

M. 281

In 1971 the building in the centre was trading as the Jenny Lass, Wade Hotel and the building was advertised as a fifteenth century royal hunting lodge that had subsequently become a hospital and chapel, before finally serving as a monastary. As it was a nineteenth century building, this rich historical pedigree was somewhat optimistic. The Jenny Lass, Wade was demolished in 1994.

St Leonard's Mill, c.1912. During the 1800s Scotland was dotted with small corn mills, many of which converted to paper production around the middle of the century to cash in on the demand from printers. To the west of St Leonard's lay the Kevock mill which began as a grain mill in the seventeenth century (also sometimes bleaching linen) and in the 1840s became a paper factory.

Although the mills and factories of the Industrial Revolution were notoriously dangerous and unpleasant to work in, there were potential benefits to be gained from organised employment even before the introduction of the Welfare State. The First Statistical Account records that 'the paper makers, carters, and colliers . . . have a fund belonging to each profession. Every person, who chooses to enter, pays so much quarterly into this common stock, and, in return, is entitled to a weekly allowance when disabled from working, by sickness or any accident'. The foundations of private health care had been laid!

LASSWADE MILL FEB 1909

Early paper manufacturing processes used linen rags from Central Europe as their raw materials, but as the process developed esparto grass (from North Africa) and wood pulp (principally from Scandinavia) became predominant. In 1909 St Leonard's was ravaged by a serious fire. Early one evening 'flames were . . . observed issuing from the top flat of the esparto grass stores' where some 300 tons of grass were stocked. Edinburgh Fire Brigade set off to the resue, but as they did not officially operate as far from the city as Lasswade they were soon called back. This fiasco, combined with the size of the fire, brought about the destruction of most of the premises.

LASSWADE FIRE. FEB. 1909.

Having caught hold of the esparto grass, the flames spread to the building's lower floors where bales of wood pulp were stored. The roof and windows quickly gave way, and the fire travelled eastwards, setting the beating and breaking houses alight. With the flames burning out of control (not to mention no fire brigade to fight them), the three-storey finishing house and store rooms finally caught light. 300 tons of paper were destroyed but two areas of the mill escaped unscathed. These were the boiler house and chimney, situated across the road from the main mill premises, and the new paper stores at the Bridgend portion of the works.

ELDIN PLACE, LASSWADE

In September 1842, Queen Victoria and Prince Albert visited Lasswade, approaching the village via Polton Road which leads on to Elm Row. But not without the sort of difficulties faced by modern drivers: 'the Royal carriage was stopped to have the drag applied . . . the road being very steep round the awkward angle'.

Polton Road is little changed. Here it is in 1911.

As the paper industry developed, smaller outfits evolved and combined to form larger mechanised mills. Paper making began at Springfield Mill in 1742, and the works were mechanised in 1816. William Tod, the farmer, flour miller and Lasswade baker who had established St Leonard's in 1843, bought Springfield Mill around 1866 and by the mid-1950s it still employed around 200. It closed in 1967.

The Polton Paper Mills Company, situated on the south bank of the Esk adjacent to Springfield Mill, was established c.1750. In 1768, a feu charter and water rights were granted to the owners by Polton Estate, and this stability prompted the building of a very extensive mill with five vats. But Polton was mismanaged and when its owners went bankrupt their assets were sold. The building and machinery fetched less than a third of its original cost. Despite these difficulties, subsequent changes of management and a serious fire in 1846, Polton survived until 1949.

BROOMIEKNOWE

With their leafy streets and grandiose villas, Broomieknowe and Hillhead illustrate the prosperity that Bonnyrigg and Lasswade were enjoying by the end of the nineteenth century. The attractions of the countryside prompted an influx of the Edinburgh upper-middle classes, and no wonder, considering the idyllic descriptions written . . . 'in the immediate neighbourhood of the beautiful village of Lasswade . . . the climate is mild, and the air soft and agreeable . . . a place of considerable resort to the inhabitants of Edinburgh and Leith, numbers of whom annually spend the summer months in this delightful locality.'

HILLHEAD, BONNYRIGG

While the villas of Broomieknowe remain intact, Hillhead on the other hand is much changed.

Bonnyrigg High Street looking towards Hillhead. In 1953 J.B. Cairns wrote provocatively that 'unlike Lasswade, Bonnyrigg has no history'. Although Bonnyrigg was originally far less well established than its neighbour, as the nineteenth century advanced coal began to be mined on a larger and more organised scale while other industries relocated to the town. As a result Bonnyrigg enjoyed a period of steady physical and economic growth at a time when its previously dominant neighbour was in decline. The relative activity of the two communities is reflected in their populations. Between 1871 and 1921 the number of people living in Bonnyrigg more than doubled but Lasswade's population fell by more than 25%.

A station on the Edinburgh to Peebles line opened adjacent to Dundas Street in Bonnyrigg in 1855, and six years later the new Esk Valley branch provided rail access into the valley itself. Of the three new stations on the branch line, Broomieknowe was on the High Street, to the left of where the two men are standing. The ornate building on the right was the premises of Henry Widnell & Son, carpet makers, who relocated to Bonnyrigg in 1868 after renewal of the lease on their Lasswade premises was refused. They also set up a plant in Roslin and went on to establish a third factory at Eskbank in 1878. By 1895 the three plants had 250 power looms between them and in 1910 employed around 850 people.

HIGH STREET, BONNYRIGG, LOOKING W.

Bonnyrigg Parish Church, originally the U.F. Church, was built in 1845. The pointed porch of the church halls is across the road, with the original Bonnyrigg Public School beside it, set back from other buildings behind railings and an arched gateway. As the roll of pupils increased, a bigger school was needed and a new building was opened in Polton Street in 1909. The old school was then turned into a picture house. This was later bought by a Mr Readshaw, who showed Midlothian's first talkie there in 1929 and later expanded the premises, building a new cinema and dance hall around the existing structure in 1939. The Regal became a bingo hall in the sixties, and after extensive modernisation was later used as a sports centre.

L.4084   HIGH STREET, BONNYRIGG

The same view showing the new Regal's distinctive art deco facade. Unfortunately for Mr Readshaw, no sooner had he modernised and extended his property, it was requisitioned by the army. For the duration of the Second World War it became the base of the Durham Light Infantry and the Border Regiment. Despite this setback, the new dance hall finally opened in 1945 and was an instant success. The cinema has since been demolished and the site acquired by Castle Rock Housing Association for a sheltered housing development.

High Street, looking North, Bonnyrigg

The view is a side street to one of the many slums in England.

This is my last photo, do I not look well? HaHa. Helen S. Keppel, Morden, Manitoba, Can

The view into High Street from Dundas Street, c.1905. Bonnyrigg Toll has been the focus of several redevelopments this century, one of the early ones being the building of the Commercial Bank, prominent in the picture opposite. This postcard was sent to someone in Iowa and states, 'the view is a side street to one of the many slums in England.'

The Commercial Bank was put up around 1925 after a fire destroyed Pringle's grocers which was the last business to occupy the old corner site. The bank has been replaced by a rather dreary three storey building. The rounded building across the road from the bank was Dick's shoe warehouse, which stood on the site of the old toll house.

1865.

DUNDAS STREET, BONNYRIGG.

Looking down Dundas Street from the toll. The two-storey building in the left foreground has been sacrificed to road widening, but the other buildings on this side of the street are intact. The Calderwood pub, adjoining the two-storey building in the middle distance, appears to have been selling liquor from the same premises for at least 100 years. Ordnance Survey maps of 1894 show the same building as the Calderwood Arms.

RAILWAY CROSSING, DUNDAS STREET, BONNYRIGG.

Bonnyrigg goods yard stood just to the right of Dundas Street at this point, and since the railway's closure in 1967 new housing at Waverley Court has been built on its site. Across the road, the former line has been turned into a walkway leading to Rosewell and Penicuik. The signal box has been removed, as have the buildings further up the street on the right.

Dundas Street, Bonnyrigg,

3557

With increasing traffic pressures, the crossroads at Bonnyrigg Toll were widened by degrees. The rounded building on the corner of High Street (see page 37), was one of the first casualties, while the two-storey block on the corner of Dundas Street above was subsequently demolished.

Polton Street looking towards the toll.

POLTON STREET, BONNYRIGG

Polton Street photographed from the junction with Dobbie's Road in 1913.

Bonnyrigg became a burgh in 1865, and with its new status acquired power to make the improvements to amenities such as street lighting that its growing prosperous population demanded. The Advertiser wrote that: 'Bonnyrigg folks are this week priding themselves on their new installation of gas lighting. Their streets are bright with the shining of 118 incandescent gas lamps, and they can journey along after nightfall without fear of tumbling over unexpected barriers. To strangers, who remember the dingy appearance of the streets after dark, the improvement appeals with particular force.'

By 1955, Bonnyrigg was being described as the 'wealthier partner' of the joint burgh, and in 1969 a commentator observed that 'beautiful houses have been built, an impressive shopping centre has been created'. As post-war urban redevelopment schemes go, Bonnyrigg got off fairly lightly, although the village charm of Polton Street was completely wiped out.

Lothian Street, Bonnyrigg.

Lothian Street looking away from the toll. The cottage on the left of this picture has been demolished and replaced by a two-storey block with shops on the ground floor and flats above. Bonnyrigg's swanky library building, opened in 1909, is now used by several different community groups.

Lothian Street. Bonnyrigg.

M. 271.

Although the tenements in the foreground of this view of Lothian Street are still intact, Bonnyrigg's war memorial has been relocated to King George V park and the entrance to Quarryfoot Gardens stands in its place.

    Ordnance Survey maps of 1894 show two old mine shafts in the vicinity of Lothian Street, one on the site of the present football ground and one in the area of Waverley Crescent.

Railway Station. Bonnyrigg.

M. 271.

In July 1855 the Peebles Railway Company opened Bonnyrigg Station. This stop seems to have been solely for goods, as a month later the North British Railway approached the owners of the line to ask if they would make provisions for a passenger station there. They offered to pay ten shillings a week towards the cost, and in response an engineer for the Peebles Railway was 'requested to get a platform shed erected, of the plainest kind, without delay.

In 1962 the Peebles line closed to passengers. Although only a single track remained, freight services operated on the line for five more years and the station remained in a state of semi-dereliction during this period.

PUBLIC PARK, BONNYRIGG

Bonnyrigg's original recreation ground was behind High Street and Polton Street and bounded by Dobbie's Road and Park Road. Sheep may have grazed there once, but this area is now wholly built up and new recreation facilities lie to the north-west at the King George V playing fields.

Bonnyrigg Town Council, apparently about to enjoy a bureaucrats' picnic at Katie's Well. One of the problems facing the burgh following its formation in 1865 was the location and establishment of an adequate water supply. The well was one of the sources investigated, although despite the quality of the water being good the supply was inadequate for burgh needs, because the tenant on Whitehill Estate [above Rosewell] had the first claim and the burgh would receive only the surplus.

Sir Walter Scott began his married life in this house at Lasswade, where he lived between 1798 and 1804. Along with other upper-class Edinburgh residents, Scott was attracted to the rural location of the village and used the house as a retreat from Auld Reekie. He was visited there by William and Dorothy Wordsworth.

THOMAS DE QUINCEY'S COTTAGE, POLTON

Another literary figure who spent time in the area was Thomas De Quincey who lived with his three daughters in this 'cottage' in Polton from 1840 to 1859. De Quincey too valued the isolation of the area but as his biography points out, 'the only drawback in the situation of the cottage was its tenuous link of communication with the nearest post office at Lasswade, a couple of miles away. De Quincy feared for his manuscripts and proofs, as mail reached the cottage by a motley selection of messengers including at times the postmistress's servant girl and a six year old boy.'

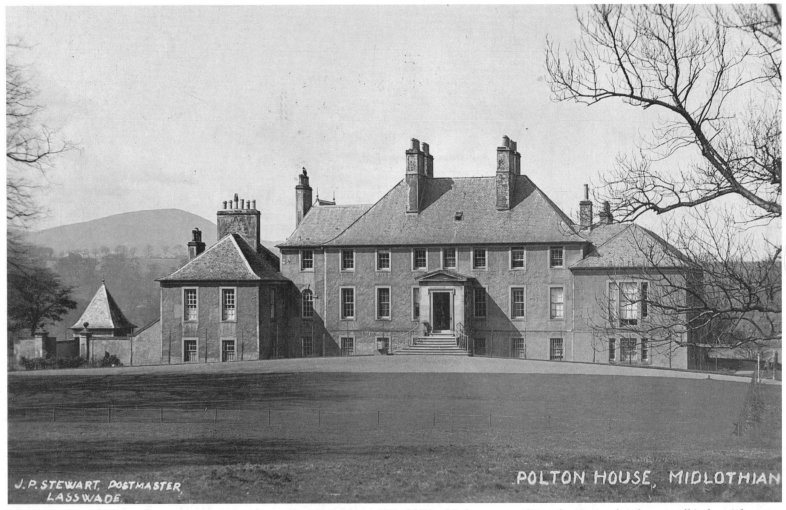

POLTON HOUSE, MIDLOTHIAN

J.P. STEWART, POSTMASTER,
LASSWADE.

Polton House was used to accomodate Jewish refugees during the Second World War. No longer standing , the site is taken by a small industrial estate.